Forest Bathing:
Living and
Healing

A Photo Journal

iUniverse books may be ordered through booksellers or by contacting:

iUniverse
1663 Liberty Drive
Bloomington, IN 47403
www.iuniverse.com
1-800-Authors (1-800-288-4677)

Because of the dynamic nature of the internet, any web addresses or links contained in this book may have changed since publication and may no longer be valid. The views expressed in this work are solely those of the author and do not necessarily reflect the views of the publisher, and the publisher hereby disclaims any responsibility for them.

ISBN: 978-1-5320-5966-7 (sc)
ISBN: 978-1-5320-5967-4 (e)
ISBN: 978-1-5320-5968-1 (hc)

Library of Congress Control Number: 2018912629

Print information available on the last page.

iUniverse rev. date: 11/28/2018

In loving memory of Violet Kathryn Ahearn, my five-year-old granddaughter, a beautiful, bright, loving child who brought joy and laughter to all who had the privilege of knowing her. On July 20, 2015, Violet was called home to heaven by her Creator.

May you be among the angels. Rest in eternal peace, beautiful child.

It is not so much for its beauty that the forest makes a claim upon men's hearts, as for that subtle something, that quality of air, that emanation from old trees, that so wonderfully changes and renews a weary spirit.

—Robert Louis Stevenson (1850–1894)

Contents

Preface

Welcome to the world of forest bathing. Get comfortable, grab a drink, and relax with a good book. That is my favorite idea of experiencing "me time." *Forest Bathing: Living and Healing, A Photo Journal* does just that … and more. Sometimes you are not able to take that walk in the forest that heals the soul and relaxes the mind.

These beautiful photographs help you virtually take a walk in the woods. Solo reading (walking) helps me solve problems, personally and professionally. It also helps me feel better, less stressed, and happier. *Solvitur ambulando*, credited to Diogenes the Cynic, translates to "it is solved by walking."

It is important to get your share of vitamin G, or green therapy, as often as you can. And this leafy therapy is right on your coffee table or shelf. As you read this book, you'll develop a relationship with the photographer. You'll live and heal, just as she planned.

Give it a read, and take that walk.

—Cecilia Ann Michalik

I found out about forest bathing less than two years ago. The spring before learning about this subject, I decided to get healthier and began to increase my activity and change my diet. Things were going well with weight loss. Then our granddaughter Violet became ill. Therapy began, and the family surrounded Violet and one another for support. Unexpectedly, I found myself, when not at the hospital, out walking. It became a daily activity that I could not stop.

Through the ups and downs of this medical nightmare, it became clear after only three weeks that our precious Violet was now in critical condition. Not understanding why, I continued to walk, exploring forests and varying trails. I had many conversations with God about Violet as I walked. And upon our profound loss of Violet, with only questions remaining, I continued to walk in the woods.

The year after Violet passed, a friend asked me to join her for a weekend retreat at Kripalu Center. Our weekend started on a Friday evening as the group sat in a circle with beautiful ambiance as we met our instructors. Our guides explained the weekend plans and made the statement that we would begin our forest bathing at nine o'clock the next morning.

I immediately turned to my friend and asked, "Are we going to be naked in the woods and take a bath?"

I did not realize why I was walking until that moment when I heard about forest bathing. This was the reason I was driven to walk, to help myself deal with the horror of Violet's passing.

The medical benefits became self-evident, and as a nurse generalist, I realized the need for more research and understanding. We took a formal forest guide session at Tower Hill with Nadine Mazzola, who explained to the group how to enjoy walking by using all our five senses. In addition, I interviewed an American Navajo chief from New Mexico.

After learning more about forest bathing, I now enjoy walking even more and plan to walk for years ahead. Friends and family have always said that they so enjoyed my photography and that I should produce a book for all to see and enjoy.

I continue to be an avid walker, traveling the world and the fifty American states, exploring new areas with beautiful natural surroundings. As a professional photographer, I always take photographs along the way. I am hoping to share my photography and my niece Lisa Zschuschen's writing expertise with others to experience forest bathing.

—Patricia Ahearn, RN BSN
Photographer

Acknowledgments

Immediately I think of our precious Violet, who left our lives tragically. Her parents and brother have supported me in sharing Violet, telling you about the joy she brought to so many people, which extends way beyond her family. She was that special. She knew it, and everyone who met her knew it. Princess of her preschool, she was in charge of every teacher and principal she met. Thank you to Violet's mom, dad, and brother.

Thanks to my beautiful family: husband, daughter, grandchildren, and extended family, who always seem to say the right thing about my pictures. They continue to encourage me to take more pictures and often have them displayed in their homes.

Thank you to my friends for supporting my photography as I share my daily walks on Facebook. One friend, who was being treated for cancer, often expressed her enjoyment of seeing the daily pictures from my walks in the woods. They provided her relief as she remained housebound recovering from very difficult therapy.

Another friend encouraged her Girl Scout troop to spend a few hours learning about forest bathing, and she allowed me to photograph their experience, hoping the joy that can be seen in the pictures and what they learned will remain with them forever.

Thanks to my dog friends, who were all willing to share their enjoyment of walking with their pets in the woods. It was so much fun for the dogs and clearly enjoyed by all.

In addition, this book would not have been possible without our dear friend Cecilia Michalik. Her guidance and support from conception to completion has been ongoing with the one goal to have a beautiful book to enjoy.

Welcome to Forest Bathing

Welcome to the world of forest bathing, a concept that dates back to at least the 1980s. Its origins are attributed to Japan, and it promises its followers relaxation, whole-body health benefits, a renewed sense of purpose, and a return to nature. Forest bathing, or *shinrin-yoku*, its Japanese name, is not a new theory. It is simply defined as walking in the woods.

Walking can provide relief in many forms. Forest bathing takes it a step further and suggests that not just walking, but walking in the woods, can be even more beneficial. According to Dr. Eva Selhub, who wrote *Your Brain on Nature* in 2012, "Individuals report that forests are the perfect landscape to cultivate what are called transcendent experiences—these are unforgettable moments of extreme happiness, of attunement to that outside the self, and moments that are ultimately perceived as very important to the individual."[1]

Since its founding in the 1980s, the concept and practice of forest bathing has expanded immensely. There are now schools and organizations that specialize in forest bathing, from the certification of therapy guides to weeklong forest bathing retreats to academic and medical studies at universities and hospitals worldwide. Later in the book, New England's first certified forest therapy guide, Nadine Mazzola, teaches about the requirements and experiences of leading a forest walk.[2]

Medical studies about forest bathing abound. Many cite the physical and emotional response to the trees themselves. According to a November 2016 *Washington Post* article,

> Some researchers attribute shinrin-yoku's health benefits to substances called Phytoncides, also called "the aroma of the forest" which are anti-microbial organic compounds given off by plants ... Another possible explanation for forest bathing's soothing effects involves our sense of awe when viewing natural beauty.[3]

In this photo journal, the authors explain, in their own words, what forest bathing has meant for them, their family, and their health. The photographs were included to showcase local natural beauty, to highlight nature in its most pristine form, through the seasons and using our five senses.

---

[1] Eva Selhub, *Your Brain on Nature* (Wiley, 2012).
[2] Nadine Mazzola, interview, May 4, 2017; additional emails and phone calls (2017–2018).
[3] Meeri Kim, "'Forest Bathing Is Latest Trend to hit U.S.'—'Where Yoga Was 30 Years Ago,'" *Washington Post*, May 17, 2016.

With commentary from residents, medical doctors, and wellness professionals, we want forest bathing to become a wonderful part of your life. Through *Forest Bathing: Living and Healing, A Photo Journal*, we hope to interest you in the benefits of forest bathing on your health and well-being and on your relationship to nature. While there are many forest therapy programs, this book will serve as an introduction to experience the benefits at home.

Forest Bathing: Medical Benefits and Validation

We didn't get too far in our research for forest bathing when first confronted with its medical and health benefits. Walking in the woods has been around since the dawn of time, but forest bathing is a bit different. What you are asked to do in forest bathing is to let go of all other thoughts, to simply "be one with nature," for a specific amount of time. The only requirement to forest bathing is your willingness to let go. It's not easy. On a recent walk, I found myself struggling with the phone in my pocket and stressed about money. I was admittedly a bit grumpy. Over time, however, a whole aura of calmness washed over me.

The practice of *shinrin-yoku* (forest bathing) is traced back to 1982 in Japan.[4] The Forest Agency of Japan "wanted to encourage a healthy lifestyle and decrease stress levels," according to Qing Li, a senior assistant professor at the Nippon Medical School in Tokyo, who is studying forest medicine. Dr. Li has conducted several experiments to test the effects of forest bathing on moods, stress levels, and the immune system. In one study, the profile of mood states (POMS) test was used to show that forest bathing trips significantly increased the score of vigor in subjects and decreased the scores for anxiety, depression, and anger.[5]

Li's studies insist that those suffering grief from loss, as well as post-traumatic stress disorder (PTSD) and cancer patients, can strongly benefit from forest bathing. His studies on immune function considered whether forest bathing increases the activity of people's natural killer (NK) cells, a part of the immune system that fights cancer. These cells provided "rapid responses" to viral-infected cells and responded to tumor formation. The increase in these cells is associated with immune system health and cancer prevention.[6]

In two studies, small groups of men and women were assessed after a two- or three-day forest bathing trip. Students walked in the woods and slept in a hotel in the woods. Blood tests showed a significant increase in NK activity. Part of the medical benefit comes from breathing air that contains phytoncides (wood essential oils). Due to his studies and their results, the Forest Agency of Japan spent millions designating forty-eight therapy trails for Japanese residents.

---

[4] Qing Li, "Forest Bathing," associated readings, YouTube videos, Wikipedia.org entries, and postings online.
[5] Ibid.
[6] Ibid.

There is pretty good evidence at least to draw an outline of a conclusion: breathing in, digging, and playing in dirt may be good for our health. Dirt has a microbiome, and it may also double as an antidepressant. Common soil bacteria is called *mycobacterium vaccae*. Soil must no longer be confused with dirt. It is a living, breathing form of nature.[7]

Some tips from Dr. Li include the following:

1. If you take an entire day forest bathing, it is better to stay in the forest for about 4 hours and walk about 3.1 miles (5 kilometers). If you take a half day forest bathing, it is better to stay about 2 hours and walk about 1.55 miles (2.5 kilometers).
2. If you want to boost your immunity (NK activity), a three-day/two-night forest bathing trip is recommended.
3. Remember that forest bathing is a preventative measure for diseases; therefore, if you come down with an illness, see a doctor, not a forest.[8]

Research institutes, medical professionals, and healthy living practitioners all agree that spending time in the woods helps your mood and can contribute to a healthier you.

A set of balance and healthy eating habits, along with the practice of *shinrin-yoku*, improves physical and mental health. Massachusetts psychotherapist Carol Santarpio, LMHC, MA, says, "Forest bathing opens you up to the serenity of nature. It is a natural healer. Many individuals report feeling a sense of calmness as nature's natural energy embraces you."[9]

Another researcher, Mark Berman, hypothesized that forest bathing or going for a walk in the woods helps people take a break from voluntary attention and thus improve cognition. He was right: the nineteen subjects, all suffering from major depressive disorder, showed significant improvements in memory span. Berman states there are many reasons why forest bathing is so good for our brains, but the most important thing, according to him, is to give the mind a chance to "wander aimlessly and be engaged—involuntarily but gently—by your surroundings."[10]

---

[7] Ibid.
[8] Ibid.
[9] Phone conversation between Carol Santarpio and Pat Ahearn, June 22, 2018.
[10] Ibid.

Native Americans and Nature's Spirituality

We are thankful to the East because everyone feels good in the morning when they awake, and sees the bright light coming from the East; and when the Sun goes down in the West we feel good and glad we are well; then we are thankful to the West. And we are thankful to the North, because when the cold winds come we are glad to have lived to see the leaves fall again; and to the South, for when the south wind blows and everything is coming up in the spring, we are glad to live to see the grass growing and everything green again. We thank the Thunders, for they are the manitous that bring the rain, which the Creator has given them power to rule over. And we thank our mother, the Earth, whom we claim as mother because the Earth carries us and everything we need.

—Charley Elkhair, quoted in M. R. Harrington, *Religion and Ceremonies of the Lenape, Indian Notes and Monographs*, Museum of the American Indian, Heye Foundation, volume 19 (1921)

Forest bathing is an activity that people of any race, gender, age, or history can appreciate. While Japan is given credit for the formal practice of forest bathing, Navajo chief Norman Tully knows all the benefits of being in the forest, for that is how he has always lived.

Based in Albuquerque, Chief Tully recently shared some thoughts and sentiments about forest bathing. Native Americans seem to possess a special knowledge and appreciation for all things nature. He says that, for most indigenous people, "time is everything" and it's important to "take a moment to be grateful."[11]

On a YouTube video, Chief Tully listed what he said were Native American Commandments. Here is the list (as many pertain to forest bathing):

- The Earth is our Mother; care for her.
- Honor all your relations.
- Open your heart and soul to the Great Spirit.
- All life is sacred; treat all beings with respect.
- Take from the earth what is needed … nothing more.
- Do what needs to be done for the good of all.
- Give constant thanks to the Great Spirit for each new day.

---

[11] Norman Tully, interview conducted by Pat Ahearn and written by Lisa Zschuschen, June 9, 2018.

- Speak the truth but only of good in others.
- Follow the rhythms of nature; rise and retire with the sun.
- Enjoy life's journey but leave no tracks.

Chief Tully spoke at great length about how forest bathing can work with anyone. It calms the spirit, and nature truly heals.

When Chief Tully prepares for ceremonies, he goes into the woods to sit with nature. He listens and talks to the birds and wind and sits next to a tree. During his journey in the woods, he will "sit by a tree and then asks the ants, trees and birds for guidance. I breathe in and out and meditate. I stay until I get the answers I need. This could be an hour or an entire day."

Including the five senses into his walks brings greater understanding of nature's impact. The following list contains his observations on incorporating the senses. Each morning, Chief Tully would awake and do the following:

- smell: fire with the odor of cedar trees, freshness of sage, cedar, and the clean air
- taste: cornmeal, wild meat, and wild berries[12]
- touch: rocks, trees, and the dirt
- see: trees, animals, and animal footprints
- hear: the echoes of your voice in the wind

Respect for all life, even the smallest creature, such as a spider or an ant, is part of their values. "Everyone picks up something good from the forest," Chief Tully said.[13]

Native Americans have a great respect for nature, and they make use of trees in practical ways as well. Trees were the original directional signs. Trail marker trees were early forms of land navigation that North America's first inhabitants created. This creative and ingenious method of shaping trees by the Native Americans marked paths in the wilderness, used by scouts and hunters, pointing to water or even the way home. Trees were the original directional signs. (Many are still in existence today and highly revered.)

---

[12] In traditional ceremonies, Chief Tully said they also eat a tablespoon of dirt.

[13] Norman Tully, interview conducted by Pat Ahearn and written by Lisa Zschuschen, June 9, 2018.

Don't Leave Your Senses Behind

....

Using all five senses while forest bathing will greatly enhance the experience. With each sense, you can truly experience the forest in a new light. Taste, touch, see, smell, and hear all the woods have to offer. Your senses will feel fresh and new after a walk through the woods.

Start by going outside. Practice in your yard. Note the green grass, feel the light wind, and smell the scent of your neighbor's barbeque. Taste the rain that's predicted to come, and hear the kids playing with their new bikes. Close your eyes and relax. Maybe take a seat in the freshly cut lawn. Take it all in.

Treat yourself to a quiet time of reflection, and enjoy the mystery of the forest. The bath will help cleanse and refresh. Take time to use all your senses, smell the rain, listen for songbirds, feel the wind blowing through the trees, touch the ragged bark of a tree, taste the sweetness of the babbling brook, and stay in the moment.

When you head to the forest, you can repeat the steps. You can begin by noticing the new sounds, tastes, smells, and so on. Here is a list of sensory activities to get started:

Sight

- Watch the flow of a river or stream as it travels over rocks.
- Notice birds flying above.
- Observe the milkweeds exploding in the wind.
- Stop and scan the woods. Do a literal 360 around you and capture all that is there.
- Find leaves, study them, and see their similarities.
- Look for acorns, seeds, and branches.

Hear

- Listen for the pitter-patter of small animals running and exploring.
- Hear the woodpecker making his mark.
- Notice the rustle of dried leaves and branches as you walk.
- Listen as the birds and bees identify their presence through song.

Touch

- Feel a soft fern, flower, crunchy leaves, or the bark of a tree.
- Touch different pinecones, and notice the differences.
- Hold some pussy willows, and feel how soft they are.
- Try to find the smoothest stone.

Taste

- Open your mouth, and savor the cool, clean air.
- Make some forest tea with safe items you've gathered.

Smell

- Inhale the distinct smell of pine trees and their needles.
- Detect the sweet fragrance of fruit trees and the musty odor after a rain shower.
- Notice the pungent scent of soil.

These are just a few ways to get your senses going. Only your imagination can limit you. Bring a journal and compare what senses you used more or less of, what you noticed, and what you did and didn't like. Forest bathe in different weather to really trick your mind. Get out and explore the world through your five senses and forest bathing.

Spring

Spring is truly a magical time. This yearly natural phenomena creates exceptional memories of rebirth and resurgence. Spring days are touched with sunshine. Spring offers hope. Spring is when rain falls from the sky, flowers begin to appear, and animals (and people) awake from hibernation and begin to live again. Spring is color. It is seeing the florals awaken. It is smelling the fresh air. It is spending more time walking, being out in nature. Spring flowers and nature are sunshine to the soul.

Tower Hill Botanic Garden, Boylston, MA.

Fiddleheads alongside streams and rivers.

Visual signs of birth.

Mushrooms are all over the forest floor, even in trees.

Estes Park, CO.

Spring is nature's way of saying "let's party." (Robin Williams)

Pike National Forest, CO.

Sprague Lake, NM.

Summer

How can one not appreciate summer? Summer is the flavors, the colors, the warmth, the kids being home, and the frolicking through fields and in the lakes and oceans. It's the simple joys of vacations and time with family and friends. Lazy, hazy summertime is the greatest.

Fight that lazy feeling, and go walk in the woods. See the fruit trees, the baby animals recently born, and the trees in all their green glory. Listen to the new (summer) sounds. Smell the freshness, the honeyed air. It's summer, and the memories are just waiting to happen.

How many faces can you see?

Enjoy the silence, the scents, sounds of birds singing, and acorns dropping.
Clear your mind.

Dancing in the wind!

Dixon, NM

Ojo Caliente, NM.

Ulysses Township, OH

Crawford Notch State Park NH.

Durango CO

Estes Park CO.

Silverton, CO

Summer transition offers new exploration and appreciation for nature. All change is a miracle to contemplate; but it is a miracle which is taking place every instant. (Henry David Thoreau, Walden Woods)

Pagosa Springs, CO

Wintrethur, DE.

Crawford Notch State Park, NH.

Sutton, MA.

Sprague Lake, CO.

Autumn

Autumn is one of the best seasons. Everywhere you look, you will see the bright colors of pumpkins, the red berries, the trees, and the flowers preparing to rest. The fall leaves provide picturesque and amazing views, especially in New England. There is a festival of fall colors everywhere. Think of the cozy autumn days and crisp fall nights. Go spend time outdoors, and witness fall in all its spectacular designs. Fall represents "turning over a new leaf."

Dean Park, Shrewsbury, MA

Wachusett Meadow (Audubon), Princeton, MA.

Kripalu. Stockbridge, MA.
There is nothing more enriching than a stroll on a crisp autumn day, filled with colors, cool breezes, and leaves gently floating to the ground.

The trails provide a musical treat under your feet, with the sound of the fallen leaves crunching/rustling as you stroll.

The vibrant trees and foliage are breathtaking.

Rail Trail West Boylston, MA.

25

Wachusett Meadow Princeton, MA (Audubon)

Winter

It's time to bundle up and go outside. See winter animals abound. Appreciate the snow and the artistic frost designs that nature provides. Forest bathing is best in winter: the crisp leaves underneath your feet, the ice on the water, and the footprints in the snow. Pay attention to the animals in winter. Note the changes in the trees and flowers. Go sledding and ice-skating. Enjoy the winter. Don't be stuck inside the house. Appreciate the depth of nature, the cold of winter, and the frosty air.

"Don't slip on the ice!"

Winter weather, snow, and the cold should not stop you from leaving your home to explore.

Artemas Ward Estate Shrewsbury, MA.

Frozen ground, lakes, and ponds accompany bare trees. This time of year provides a magical time in the forest.

Crizzle is the sound and action of open waters as it freezes.

Snowy mornings create warm memories.

"We feel cold, but we don't mind it, because we will not come to harm. And if we wrap up against the cold, we wouldn't feel other things, like the tingle of the stars, or the music of the aurora, or best of all, the silky feeling of moonlight on our skin. It's worth being cold for that." (Philip Pullman, *The Golden* Compass).

Sutton, MA.

Living

What does it mean to really be alive? How does one truly find pleasure from daily life? Long days and the stresses of family, work, friends, and commitments can take their toll. But to be alive? To not just exist and survive but to be living, present, and open? That is the true struggle.

Living can mean entirely different things to different people. Living is, by definition, sometimes enough. Being alive is all some of us need. But *alive* and *living* are two separate words with separate meanings. One can be alive but not truly living. Celebrate life with walks in nature. Enjoy the challenges and health benefits of fresh air—walking, climbing, and experiencing life before concrete, bricks, and asphalt.

In this section, the author wants to inspire us all to live and to be awake, refreshed, and recharged.

Forest bathing can be the perfect engine for us all to begin living again. Taking simple walks can have profound effects on our physical health, minds, and spirits. Being in the woods, sometimes referred to as "nature's playground," can offer so many lessons on living, lessons that can be imparted to our children and the elderly. Living is something we must all remember to do. Cognitively, we must remind ourselves how lucky we are, how quickly things can change, and how life can be snatched away. Nature reminds us all the time.

There is a peace, a joy, and a happiness in the forest. Embrace it. Give thanks.

Showing love to the trees with their hugs.

Young girls on a scouting trip learning the importance of forest bathing.

Franklin State Forest Franklin, MA.

Exploring nature alone or with loved ones, teaching children the value in exploring the woods can give a lifetime of skills for the future.

"Children are great imitators. So give them something great
to imitate." (Anonymous)

Walking and enjoying nature with all of your senses.

Have an encounter with nature.

Find your secret space in the woods.

Purgatory Chasm Sutton, MA.

Parker, CO.

"I am going forest bathing."

Crawford Notch State Park, NH.

Healing

The word *healing* is often associated with negative connotations. Healing means one must have recovered from something. Healing is what happens after one is physically or emotionally broken. With forest bathing, however, one can see that healing can represent an idea altogether different and refreshing. To heal, one can move on, start anew, and begin life again. Just saying the word or phrase can be life-affirming.

By definition (dictionary.com), *heal* means "to make healthy, whole, or sound; restore to health; free from ailment," among several other things. With forest bathing, the forest, including nature in all its forms like trees, grasses, wood, water, animals, and so on, is the healer. After forest bathing, one can be healed from sin, injury, trauma, and distress.

But the trees can also build one up, restore you to your former self, and show you greater joy. People often comment that an injury or event changes them, so much so that they feel recharged and appreciate life again. What a shame that one must experience pain to feel joy. No more! With forest bathing, each of us can begin the day fully charged, ready to take on the world.

The actual biological effect of forest bathing, being among the trees, is proven. Hundreds of studies in the United States and abroad have brought healing into the forefront. No longer do people have to be in the dark, feeling left alone. The philosopher Hippocrates said it best, "Healing is a matter of time, but it is sometimes also a matter of opportunity."

Step into a new mind-set. Regain your self-esteem and worth. Come into the woods, bathe in the forest, and let the healing begin.

Tower Hill Botanic Garden
Boylston, MA.
One of the most important benefits of forest bathing is healing! These beautiful women are all in remission from cancer.

In memory of Bev who enjoyed times spent in nature.

Supporting each other in the comfort of the forest.

Being alone in the forest helps people with chronic illness, providing calmness and building your immune system by being close to the trees that emit phytoncide, proven to aid in healing.

Colton Point State Park, PA.
A veteran reveals that he finds walking in the woods is very calming. It's something bigger than one's self.

Colton Point State Park, PA.
There is nothing more tragic than the loss of a child. Healing from
the calmness of the forest helps.

Forest Bathing: Pathway to Living and Healing—Simple Reference Guide

Step One (Daily Nutrition)

- Walk daily close to home.
- Enjoy birds, pets, garden, blue sky, and fresh air.

Step Two (Reduce Stress and Cleanse)

- Walk weekly at a local park, pond, or waterway.
- Stretch, take deep breaths, and exhale.
- Disconnect from technology.

Step Three (Relax and Reduce Anxiety)

- Walk monthly with immersion into a forest.
- Ramble. Do not hike. Build body sense/ awareness.
- Smell the soil.

Step Four (Detox and Improve Immune System)

- Annually take a wilderness escape/expand experience.
- Leverage all the senses to stimulate respiration and bolster immune system.

Forest Bathing with Dogs

One of the components of forest bathing that makes it so universal is that anyone and anywhere can feel its effects. Even with ten or fifteen minutes outside, one can reap nature's benefits. The same can be said of being with our pets and companion animals.

In this forest bathing journey, the photographer had the ability to observe a forest bathing outing with dogs. Woof! Woof! Officially titled "Forest Bathing for Dog Owners" and run by Nadine Mazzola through Tower Hill Botanical Garden (as well as other places), the class delivers for both owner and dog. As dog owners and lovers, she noted that "we all want to be with our dogs."

Through forest bathing, dogs are completely in their element, using their sense of smell and love for the natural world. They are born explorers. They will stop and obtain pleasure from the leaves, the trees, and the animals. On her website (nenft.com) and in further discussion, Mazzola explained that dogs can "act as a guide" for their owners and that dogs are "reminding us and inspiring us to be in our senses" on the walk.[14]

Bond with your dog as you enjoy the companionship and benefits of walking in the forest, and thank him for the unconditional love he gives you every day.

---

[14] Nadine Mazzola, interview, May 4, 2017; additional emails and phone calls (2017–2018).

A man and his dog on a wooden path provide much joy and exercise.

Animals love to be outside in nature exploring with their masters.

Dogs provide motivation to enjoy nature and share in their love.

Even cats enjoy being outside in nature.

Nature's Surprise

Let the games begin! With eyes wide open, walk softly, and listen closely. Now you will be included in nature's scavenger hunt.

Rules: no technology! Embrace the forest with a deep breath. Welcome the happiness and energy. And enjoy the exploration.

Nature has a sense of humor. Just look at it. The more time one spends outdoors, the more one finds reasons to laugh. From its custom of changing before one's eyes, to animals hiding behind objects, to horizons and landscapes completely changed by natural disaster or weather event, be entertained by nature. It is everywhere, especially through social media and animals being cheeky, seemingly posing for the camera.

Could it be that animals have greater intelligence than we think? Do they understand humor? How is it that certain shapes and colors, like hearts, can appear when we most need it? Nature will surprise you with an acorn man, hearts, the musk of soil, the chirp of a bird, or the rustle of leaves. What is your surprise?

Who is writing this chapter? Nature! That's who.

Oh, and by the way, do walk softly in the early morning or at night as trees do sleep!

Tower Hill, Boylston, MA

Beavers ongoing work to remove this tree but despite lack of success he continued to try over and over again.

This is the largest and oldest black oak tree in MA. Was born around 1800 and identified by Robert; a member of the Grafton Lions Club; Grafton, MA.

Washington Park Providence, RI.

The forest provides many natural gifts. The hearts are made of snow, leaves, tree trunk, flower petals, stone and grass. The forest shows love is all around us.

Manitou Springs, CO.

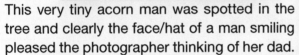

This very tiny acorn man was spotted in the tree and clearly the face/hat of a man smiling pleased the photographer thinking of her dad.

You can even forest bathe in the middle of Manhattan, NY.

The roots of this tree have captured large stones pulling them close to the tree, now prisoner and unable to escape.

Chama, NM.

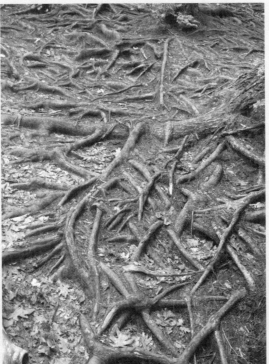

These strong trees pushed their way right in the middle of large boulders to survive and grow strong.

Estes Park, CO.

Shinrin-Yoku (Forest Bathing) with Nadine

On a picture-perfect spring day in New England, the authors were treated to an official forest bathing walk and afternoon at Tower Hill Botanical Garden in Boylston, Massachusetts. The walk was led by Nadine Mazzola, the first certified forest therapy guide in New England. After a lengthy training and certification process, Nadine realized one of her passions was nature, being outside, gardening, growing food, and teaching others how to appreciate the forest.

During our nearly three-hour walk, Nadine led us in a series of intentions that helped focus our six-person group. At fifteen- to twenty-minute intervals, after walking short distances, we would each stop and choose an image or pick up a fallen leaf or sit on a tree stump and quietly reflect on the discussion point. The intentions are based, in part, on the five senses (see, touch, taste, hear, and smell) and how the forest reignites one's senses.

At the end of the twenty-minute interval, we would gather in a circle and speak about that specific intention, for example, smell and so on. Examples include:

- *Gratitude*: "Close your eyes and stop to reflect on what in your life you feel gratitude for."
- *What's in Motion*: "What is the pace of nature? What things are moving near you?"
- *Close Gazing*: Find something nearby that is fairly small, no more than the size of a grapefruit. Give it your full attention. What about this object stands out to you?

You can do this sort of reflection anywhere, but there's more and more data that suggest reflecting in nature is how one is best served. Even without much time, there are benefits to going for short forest walks. Some suggest the forest emits vitamin K, which is essentially vitamin green.

Others shared their stories: the relaxation, the loss of anxiety, and reconnect with nature. The time flew by. Our group unanimously agreed that the walk was relaxing and that the benefits of forest bathing were obvious. It helped me to focus on the present, on the right here and now, and to not worry about the past, that which you cannot change, or the future, that which is unknown.

After our last reflection, Nadine led us to a circle and began to close the day. We watched as she unrolled a delicate tea set and saw the tiny mugs. She spun herself and began to list ingredients that she gathered as we had walked. She had a small thermos with water and a Coleman propane stove. She boiled the water. Then she turned off the water and steeped the white pine needles, wintergreen leaves, dandelion petals, violet flowers, and forsythia flowers. After steeping, we all drank the tea, which fulfilled the last unused sense, taste. We began to pack.

Nobody rushed. We all rose and slowly prepared for our reentry into the real world.[15]

Tower Hill Boylston MA.

---

[15] Ibid.

During the walk, forest items were gathered by Nadine. At the end of the walk, natures gifts were used to make forest tea; completing the fifth sense (taste).

Recipe for Forest Tea

While walking along the woods, you can pick up safe edible plants to make forest tea. The list of some of the safe plants includes the following:

- white pine needles
- wintergreen leaves
- dandelion petals
- violet flowers and leaves
- forsythia flowers
- blueberry leaves and berries
- raspberry or blackberry leaves and berries

The most important rule for collecting the plants is to be 110 percent sure that what is gathered is safe to eat. When ready to make the forest tea, boil water in a small portable camp cooking system. Or bring some hot water in a vacuum-insulated thermos.

Steep your ingredients by boiling the water and shutting off the heat source, or take the hot water thermos and add the forest plants. Steep the plants for twenty to thirty minutes as time allows. (Again be 110 percent sure of what you forage in the forest to be safe.)[16]

---

[16] Information provided by Nadine Mazzola, certified forest therapy guide, trainer, and mentor; http://www.growforagecookferment.com/foraging-for-pine-needles; https://davesgarden.com/guides/articles/view/3126.

Charlie

My favorite reflection was one where I met a monster of a moss-covered pine tree. He told me that his name was Charlie and that he had fallen over. At a distance, the ground appeared to hold three separate pine trees. On closer inspection, however, it was apparent that there was only one tree and that several new trees were growing out of its trunk. This, to me, represented new life from old. I have struggled with many things in life, but I can always begin anew.

I spent time with Charlie. We had a conversation. I spoke to him about my world, and I learned his. He taught me that, yes, we all fall, but we can regrow and begin anew. I needed that. Charlie pushed me onward. He opened my eyes to the possibilities in nature and taught me I can start again.

Since my conversation with Charlie, my outlook has changed. I realize that life is short and we must make the most of our time here.

I recently went back to see Charlie about three months after first meeting him. The moss continues to grow, but now there's a new addition—flowers! Charlie, this massive pine tree that had fallen in the woods, was springing with life, moss and flowers. It was a beautiful sight to see.

Safety Tips and Forest Etiquette

When embarking on any new adventure, it is important to use one's intuition and common sense for safety. Walking in the woods presents a situation in which safety is crucial. Also, for outdoor explorers, the creed is "leave it better than you found it." Here is a list of safety tips and forest etiquette. The following list depends on the length and time of your forest bathing walk.

Safety Tips

- Make sure at least one person knows your location and the length of your trip. Bring a fully charged phone.
- Walk with a partner for the first couple of trips.
- Always wear appropriate clothing: bring extra socks, rainwear, and a warm jacket or sweater.
- Avoid going off trail. Do not directly approach animals.
- Do not forage unless you are 100 percent certain of the plant, leaf, berry, or other specimen.
- Bring bug spray that repels ticks. (Ticks for All is an organic blend that smells great and really works.)
- Bring suntan lotion, water, snacks, flashlight, whistle, and a first-aid kit. (Other possible items include sanitizing wipes, Ziploc bags for samples, trail map, compass, emergency blanket, and water purification tablets.)

Forest Etiquette

- Take out whatever trash you bring (and more).
- Leave the land as it was intended, leaving only your footprint.
- Do not disturb wildlife or their shelter (birds' nests, approaching deer, and no pink lady slippers) as it may be illegal.
- Maintain the tranquility of the forestry cove.

Reflections by Photographer Patricia Ahearn

Forest bathing knows no season and can be taken as frequently as needed to help soothe the soul and heal the body. It is free and can be used in conjunction with family, friends, lovers, or just yourself. It is the perfect prescription for healing.

Nature is a great way to connect to your authentic self. The trees and flowers don't care how much money you make, your gender, or your race. Nature allows you to be free of life's pressures.

Nearly every morning, I go to the attic. Nearly every morning I go to the attic to blow the stuffy air out of my lungs, from my favorite spot on the floor I look up at the blue sky and the bare chestnut tree, on whose branches little raindrops shine, appearing like silver, and at the sea gulls and other birds as they glide on the wind … As long as this exists, I thought, and I may live to see it, this sunshine, the cloudless skies, while this lasts I cannot be unhappy. As long as this exists, and that should be forever, I know that there will be solace for every sorrow, whatever the circumstances. I firmly believe that nature can bring comfort to all who suffer. (Anne Frank [February 23, 1944])

Bibliography

Association of Nature and Forest Therapy Guides and Programs. "10 Forest Therapy Invitations." Anftg.org.

Astorino, Dominique Michelle. "The Wellness Trend from Japan You Need to Know About." https://www.popsugar.com/fitness/What-Forest-Bathing-42692033.

Boyce, Barry. "A Moment of Awe." Mindful 5 (3), August 2017.

Cole, Pam, and Carol Santarpio. Interviews, May 2017–June 2018.

Coy, Kelsey. "Forest Walking—Can a Walk in the Forest Make You Healthier, Happier and Smarter?" http://naturalsociety.com/forest-bathing-healthier-happier-smarter.

Kim, Meeri. "'Forest bathing' is latest trend to hit U.S.—'Where yoga was 30 years ago.'" *Washington Post*, May 17, 2016. https://www.washingtonpost.com/news/to-your-health/wp/2016/05/17/forest-bathing-is-latest-fitness-trend-to-hit-u-s-where-yoga-was-30-years-ago.

Li, Qing. "Forest bathing." Associated readings, YouTube videos, Wikipedia.org entries, and postings online, 2008–2016.

Nawrocki, Denell. "The Experience of Guiding a Single Person: A Reflection." http://www.natureandforesttherapy.org/uploads/8/1/4/4/8144400/experienceguidingasingleindividual_1_.pdf.

Mazzola, Nadine. "An Introduction to Forest Bathing: Walk and Discussion." Tower Hill Botanical Society, West Boylston, Mass. April 28, 2017.

———. Interview, May 4, 2017.

Mother Earth News. "Your Brain on Nature: Forest bathing and Reduced Stress." www.motherearthnews.com/natural-health/herbal-remedies/forest-bathing-ze0z1301zgar.

Selhub, Eva, and Alan Logan. *Your Brain on Nature*. Wiley, 2012.

Tulley, Norman. Interview conducted by Pat Ahearn and written by Lisa Zschuschen, June 9, 2018.

US National Library of Medicine, US Department of Health and Human Services, National Institutes of Health, Medline Plus. https://medlineplus.gov/news/fullstory_163189.html.

"Words for Fall." https://www.words-to-use.com/words/fall.

"Words for Winter." https://www.words-to-use.com/words/winter.

"Words for Spring." https://www.words-to-use.com/words/spring.

"Words for Summer." https://www.words-to-use.com/words/summer.

About the Authors

Patricia Ahearn

Patricia Ahearn is a grandmother, mother, wife, aunt, and sister. She enjoyed thirty-two years in a rewarding career as a registered nurse. She has a history of always being a caregiver to her family and friends. Additionally, she has taught CPR and first aid for thirty years to thousands of students.

In addition to her nursing career, she is a photographer, traveler, and avid walker. Nature has always been a part of her life. As she traveled around the world and explored the United States, she captured her trips with pictures that she shared with friends and family. A visit to Pat's house always includes photo albums.

Photography was one of the most enjoyable part of her trips. Family, friends, colleagues, and neighbors have said that she has a very special eye that captures nature in a way that brings nature to a person who may not be physically able to go outside. As she posted and shared her pictures online, she was often encouraged to make a coffee table book that would bring nature to all.

At a weekend yoga retreat, Pat heard the term "forest bathing" for the first time. After researching further, this book idea was born.

Patricia and her family experienced the tragic loss of their granddaughter, Violet. She soon realized that walking alone in the woods became therapy to cope with Violet's illness and eventual loss.

Paired together with the words of her niece, Lisa Zschuschen, this coffee table book is a dream come true for the duo.

Lisa Zschuschen

Lisa Zschuschen is a Shrewsbury, Massachusetts, native who graduated from Northeastern with a major in journalism and a minor in international affairs. She has been a writer her entire life, and her work has been featured in media such as the *Boston Globe West Weekly* and Softwaremag.com. She has traveled extensively, visiting more than thirty countries with dreams to visit many more.

Throughout her adult life, Lisa has struggled with severe depression and anxiety and deals with addiction and recovery issues. It is an ongoing struggle. However, through grit, hard work, and family support, Lisa has persevered. Forest bathing has helped immensely. This year of research has made her a student of *shirin-yoku*. With its natural soothing effects, trees bring great comfort. Lisa highly recommends forest bathing for people interested in nature, those affected by tragedy, or anyone who loves life!

Together with her aunt, Patricia Ahearn, photographer extraordinaire, Lisa is proud to author *Forest Bathing: Living and Healing.*

CPSIA information can be obtained at www.ICGtesting.com
Printed in the USA
BVIW120838211218
535826BV00001B/1